Hot hens

It is hot. Nan is thinking of food. Pop is sitting on a stool with a cool drink.

At noon, Nan tells Pop,
"I will poach the eggs and
we can have them on toast."

Pop runs to the chicken coop. He yells, "No eggs, Nan. The hens are too hot!"

"I will help the hens to get cool. Then we will get eggs," Pop tells Nan.

Pop fills a box
with lots of things.

He brings the box to
the chicken coop and
gets on with the job.

Pop tells the hens of his
plan to get them cool.

8

Pop grins and tells Nan,
"The hens will be cool."

The hens hop up on to
the roof of the chicken coop.

Nan peeks at the hens.

The hens slip and zoom.
The hens flap, splash and
cluck. They get cool.

13

The hens go back into
the chicken coop to rest.

Pop peeks into the coop and sees six eggs. He scoops them up.

Nan has lots of eggs
from her cool hens!

Words to blend

thinking	sitting	tells
need	will	poach
toast	chicken	yells
fills	box	things
brings	job	cluck
peeks	splash	back

Before reading

Synopsis: It is a hot day. Even the hens are hot. So Pop builds them a water slide because cool hens lay eggs and that's what Nan wants to cook.

Review phoneme/s: th ch ng sh ai ee igh oa oo

New phoneme: oo

Story discussion: Look at the cover, and read the title together. Ask: *Why do you think the hens are hot? Do they look happy? What do you think will happen in this story?*

Link to prior learning: Display the grapheme oo. Say: *These two letters are a digraph, that means they make one sound together. The digraph oo can make two different sounds, as in* look *and as in* food. *In this book, we're thinking about the /oo/ sound as in* food. How quickly can children find and read an oo word in the story?

Vocabulary check: Coop – a hut or pen for chickens. Ask: *Can you think of any other special names for animal houses?* (e.g. hutch, pen, nest, cage, tank)

Decoding practice: Display the words *food, book, zoom, loop, cool, mood, took, wood, foot.* Ask children to read the words and group them according to the way the oo is pronounced.

Tricky word practice: Display the word *have.* Ask children to circle the tricky part of this word (ve, which makes a /v/ sound. The e is silent.) Encourage children to practise writing this tricky word and look out for it when they are reading.

After reading

Apply learning: *Ask children what they thought of Pop's plan to help the hens cool down. Did they guess what he would do? Ask:* Do you think the hens are having fun on page 13?

Comprehension

- *Why aren't there any eggs at first?*

- *What does Pop do to solve the problem?*

- *How do you think Nan feels at the end of the story? How might the hens be feeling?*

Fluency

- *Pick a page that most of the group read quite easily. Ask them to reread it with pace and expression. Model how to do this if necessary.*

- *Turn to page 7. Ask children to read this longer sentence as fluently as possible, so the meaning is clear. Demonstrate this if necessary.*

- *Practise reading the words on page 17.*

Tricky words review

of	the	have
no	are	was
to	be	they
into	he	her
has	we	too